CW00544747

Britain
Since the War

Usborne Quicklinks

The Usborne Quicklinks website is packed with thousands of links to all the best websites on the internet. The websites include information, video clips, sounds, games and animations that support and enhance the information in Usborne internet-linked books.

To visit the recommended websites for this book, go to the Usborne Quicklinks website at **www.usborne.com/quicklinks** and enter the keywords **Post-war Britain**.

When using the internet please follow the internet safety guidelines displayed on the Usborne Quicklinks website. The recommended websites at Usborne Quicklinks are regularly reviewed and updated, but Usborne Publishing Ltd. is not responsible for the content or availability of any website other than its own. We recommend that children are supervised while using the internet.

USBORNE HISTORY OF BRITAIN

Britain
Since the War

Henry Brook & Conrad Mason

Illustrated by Ian McNee

Designed by Tom Lalonde

Edited by Ruth Brocklehurst & Jane Chisholm

Consultant: Dr. Peter Mandler,
University of Cambridge

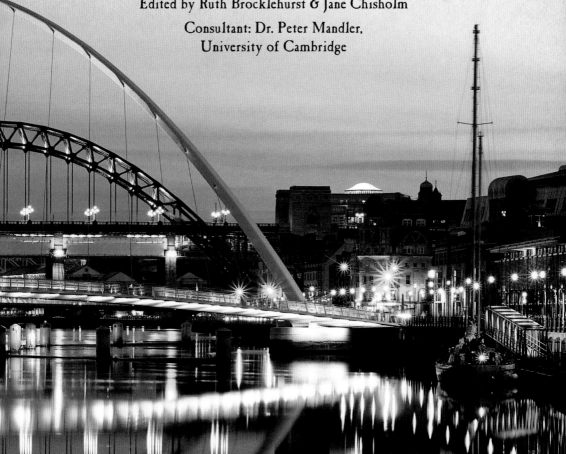

Contents

Post-war Britain

The British people had endured years of sacrifice during the Second World War, so when peace came they wanted comfortable homes, well-paid jobs and a better way of life. While politicians worked to rebuild the country, old industries fell into decline and the colonial empire that had provided wealth and global status for centuries broke apart.

The nation struggled to find its place in a changing world, as immigration from former colonies and new rights for women and minority groups made life in Britain fairer, richer and more diverse than ever before.

Advance, Britannia

After five agonizing years of war, the people of Britain spilled onto the streets on May 8, 1945, to celebrate one of the greatest triumphs in their nation's history – VE Day, Victory in Europe. The German army, which had come so close to destroying their homes and their way of life, had at last been crushed.

Men and women from all backgrounds had fought shoulder-to-shoulder to defend their country, and they looked forward to a brighter future.

"We may allow ourselves a brief period of rejoicing; but let us not forget for a moment the toil and efforts that lie ahead ... Advance, Britannia!"

Winston Churchill announces the end of the war with Germany. He was already 70 years old, but his speeches could still electrify a crowd.

Cheering crowds party in the streets of London on VE Day.

MJ 6182

The people decide

The British Prime Minister, Winston Churchill, had done more than anyone to steer the country through the dangerous war years. So, when he called an election only weeks after VE day, he was confident that voters would choose his Conservative Party. He was stunned by the result – a landslide win for the Labour Party.

This poster helped the Labour Party to win the 1945 election.

Heaven on Earth

Labour pledged to end the miseries that had plagued the country for centuries: poverty, bad housing and lack of proper medical care. The party leader, Clement Attlee, talked of building a 'New Jerusalem' – a paradise for the British people – in a reference to a patriotic song.

Attlee had embraced the ideas of William Beveridge, an economist who proposed a social care system, or 'Welfare State', that would offer government support to individuals at every stage of their lives, from "cradle to grave". Labour went further than Beveridge, promising a free National Health Service, jobs for all, millions of new houses and 'nationalization' of struggling industries, bringing them under state control. It was an ambitious plan for a better Britain, and the public backed it.

Quiet revolutionary

If Winston Churchill was a political lion, then Clement Attlee was as quiet as a mouse – supposedly described by Churchill as, "a modest little man with a lot to be modest about".

One story goes that Clement Attlee was so nervous when he met King George VI to be appointed Prime Minister that he was silent for several minutes. "I've won the election," he finally announced. "I know," replied the King, "I heard it on the news".

Global guardian

Attlee had the hopes of the nation on his shoulders, but Britain had huge international responsibilities too. Around the world, many people in Britain's vast empire were calling for change, and relying on the new government to grant them greater independence.

In the Far East, the war was still raging against Germany's last remaining ally, Japan. It would be months before some British servicemen came home.

7

Bitter recovery

The first job for Attlee's government was to rebuild and revive a war-ravaged country. Britain's cities, factories, merchant fleet and railway network were bomb-blasted and crumbling and most of the nation's wealth had been spent on the war. People of all ages and occupations looked tired and haggard after the years of turmoil and hard work. All around them were stark reminders of the high price they had paid for victory.

> "I have no easy words for the nation ... I cannot say when we shall emerge into easier times."
>
> Clement Attlee issues a sober message to Parliament in 1947.

A costly peace

Three months after VE Day, an American plane dropped an atomic bomb on Japan. Japan's leaders surrendered on August 15, 1945. This date, known as VJ Day, marked the end of the Second World War.

Church bells and ship sirens rang out across Britain as communities lit bonfires and held street parties. But, the mood of celebration was more subdued than VE Day. People had hoped life would get easier when peace came – but instead things seemed tougher than ever.

Something fishy

Fresh meat was always in short supply at this time. So government officials encouraged the public to eat horse flesh and whale steak – which was rubbery and tasted like cod liver oil.

The government also imported millions of cans of snoek – a pungent, oily fish from South Africa. People turned their noses up at snoek and most of it was mashed into pet food.

Going hungry

In 1940, the government had introduced rationing to preserve stocks of food, textiles and fuel. Shoppers exchanged coupons for a weekly basket of goods. People had tolerated these strict controls during wartime but when the war ended the country was still starved of supplies. Bread was added to the ration list in 1946 and luxuries such as new clothes, magazines, sweets and perfume were difficult to find. The British public were dismayed by these lingering hardships, but rationing continued until 1954.

Cap in hand

Shop shelves were empty and so were the government's bank vaults. It had been an expensive war and the nation had only survived thanks to donations of vital materials from America. These stopped abruptly after VJ Day so Attlee sent his top financial expert – John Maynard Keynes – to Washington, to ask the Americans for a cash gift. Keynes returned with a huge loan that saved the economy in the short term, but which wasn't paid off until 2006.

The Big Freeze

In February 1947, Britain was hit by the coldest weather in living memory. Deep snowdrifts cut off villages and trapped trains between stations. Farm animals left out in the fields froze to death, and factories and power stations ran short of coal. Struggling with rationing, debt, snow and ice, people could only grit their teeth and look forward to better times.

A big thaw

During the Big Freeze of 1947, Britain was subjected to heavy snow and temperatures as low as -21°C (-6°F).

Temperatures rose in mid-March, bringing even more misery. Ice and snow melted rapidly, causing terrible flooding which was made even worse by severe gales and torrential rains.

As water levels rose, police and the armed forces had to rescue many people from their waterlogged homes.

A family wheels home a load of coal during the winter of 1947.

No wonder they're smiling – coal was hard to come by, and domestic electricity supplies were regularly cut off for several hours at a time.

Homes for heroes

Flat-pack palaces

This photograph shows 'prefabs' – prefabricated houses – being unloaded from trucks.

Some people dismissed prefabs as ugly rabbit hutches or sardine tins. But they were snug, clean and came equipped with fridges, full-size baths and kitchen cupboards.

Many families became very attached to these new homes. The politician Neil Kinnock said that spending his childhood in a prefab was like living in a spaceship.

British soldiers were praised as heroes, but most of them came home to join their families living in run-down and crowded rooms with few of the comforts we enjoy today – like electricity, hot water and private bathrooms.

Even before the war there hadn't been enough houses to go around. Building projects had stopped during the fighting and millions of homes had been damaged or destroyed by German bombs. Now, the government ordered a frenzy of construction that dramatically changed the look of Britain's towns and cities.

Prefabulous

Brick houses would be slow to build, but the government quickly provided thousands of homes in the form of 'prefabs'. These boxy bungalows were assembled using light panels that were made in advance, or prefabricated, in former aircraft factories. They could be slotted together in a day or two.

Boom times

Although some prefabs are still standing today, they were only designed to last for around ten years. Permanent homes were needed urgently, and the demand was growing.

After the trauma and upheaval of the war, people were anxious to get on with family life. More than 400,000 couples got married in 1947. What followed became known as the 'baby boom'. A million more babies were born in the five years after the war, than had been born in the five years before the war.

Families on low incomes were the worst affected by the housing shortage. They couldn't afford to buy their own homes, so the government asked local councils to build houses for families to rent. A typical council house had three bedrooms, an indoor bathroom and lots of storage space.

The high life

Council houses offered many families a big improvement in living standards, but they were often built in large estates, packed closely together. These alarmed some politicians, who claimed they split communities into rich and poor.

Architects and planners didn't have enough land to build houses for everyone. So they also built tower blocks of flats, up to 30 floors high, in order to squeeze as many homes as possible into Britain's crowded cities.

By the end of the 1960s, the housing crisis was over – but, at a price. Many tower blocks had been cheaply built and poorly planned. They earned a reputation for being deprived and crime-infested places to live.

All mod cons

Immediately after the war, many people were trapped living in dirty city slums.

Lots of children had to share beds with their siblings, and most people had to bathe in tin tubs and use outside toilets.

Only wealthy families could afford to have central heating or refrigerators and washing machines in their homes.

By the mid-1950s, these modern conveniences, or 'mod cons', were much more widely available. Even so, by 1960 only around one in five households had a fridge.

This illustration comes from a 1951 advert for fridges.

OLYMPIC GAMES

29 JULY 1948 14 AUGUST
LONDON

'Austerity Games'

The 1948 Olympics is often referred to as the 'Austerity Games' because it was staged on a very tight budget.

Competitors were asked to bring their own towels, and many wore homemade kits.

The London athletes were given a packed lunch to get them through each day's training – a cheese sandwich, an apple and a boiled egg.

Olympians earned nothing from sport in the 1940s and many British contestants had jobs in offices and factories. They had to ask for time off work, and some even had their wages stopped.

Unity and division

In July 1948, the eyes of the world turned to London for the first Olympic Games in twelve years. After years of war, British organizers were determined that the London Olympics would be a beacon of international peace and teamwork.

Sport for all

King George VI welcomed the world's athletes to a war-bruised and rather shabby London, for an Olympic Games that was put together on a shoestring budget. Competitors brought their own food, trained in overcrowded public swimming pools and rode on packed Underground trains to Wembley Stadium.

But the event was a dazzling success. Everyone involved had pitched in to help, and the sporting spirit of the Olympics shone through.

The Iron Curtain

However, while almost 60 countries entered the Olympics, the Soviet Union was not among them. Britain, America and the Soviets had fought together during the war. But tensions were growing between the former allies in a clash of politics and beliefs that became known as the Cold War.

Soviet troops had swept across eastern Europe in the course of the war. When the fighting ended, they took control of the countries they occupied and fortified the borders. In 1946, Churchill described this new frontier as an "iron curtain" across central Europe. He and other western politicians were alarmed by the Soviet Union's growing military strength, and worried that trouble brewing in Berlin might spark another war.

Berlin under siege

At the end of the war, Germany had been carved into four zones, each governed by one of the four main allies – America, France, and Britain in the West, and the Soviet Union in the East. The German capital, Berlin, was also shared between them, but it was located deep within Soviet-run East Germany. In June 1948, the Soviets tried to dislodge the western allies by setting up a blockade. They closed all the roads, railways and waterways, planning to starve the two million people living in West Berlin into accepting Soviet rule.

Sky cargo

Britain and America refused to abandon the city. In June 1948, they launched the Berlin Airlift, flying coal, medicines and food to West Berlin in a vast fleet of cargo planes. In a joint operation lasting more than a year, the British RAF and the US Air Force flew more than a thousand flights a day – until the Soviets grudgingly re-opened the city's supply routes. But Berlin would remain a dangerous and divided city for another 40 years.

WEST GERMANY

■ NATO countries
■ Under Soviet Union control
Neutral countries

Fearing a military strike by the Soviets, Britain, America and ten other nations set up the North Atlantic Treaty Organization (NATO) in 1949.

NATO members agreed to fight together if any member country was attacked. This military alliance acted as a wall across Europe to stop any Soviet advance.

German children cheer a US cargo plane as it flies over West Berlin during the airlift.

Some pilots dropped sweets from their planes, using handkerchiefs as parachutes.

Sunset over the empire

Keeping the peace

In 1919 a panel of countries had established the League of Nations to promote international peace and justice.

After its failure to prevent the Second World War, the League reformed as the United Nations (UN) in 1945.

At its peak, the British empire covered one quarter of the world's land and for centuries it was a reminder of Britain's superpower status. But, after the turmoil of two world wars, it had become a costly burden and people at home and abroad wanted independence for the colonies. The government started to untangle Britain's overseas ties and responsibilities and, before long, the empire vanished from the maps.

A jewel in the East

With its cotton, tea and precious gemstones, India had been a prized and closely guarded colony throughout Victorian times. But, by the 1940s, the country was in chaos and on the brink of civil war. Although the Indian people had been calling for independence for decades, rival religious groups among them had very different visions for the future.

British officials struggled to arrange a peaceful transfer of power, but in 1947 they were forced to split the land in two. The southern part kept the name of India and became a new independent state; the northern part became a separate Muslim country called Pakistan. Millions of people had to leave their homes to join their religious communities, and many thousands died in violence along the border.

UN troops act as peacekeepers in war zones worldwide. They wear baby blue berets and helmets.

NATIONS UNIES

This poster from 1947 promotes the UN as a tree of peace, with the flags of member nations as its leaves.

No peace for Palestine

After the First World War, the League of Nations had appointed Britain to govern several territories in the Middle East. These included Palestine, where the British government had promised land to Jews from around the world to build a new nation.

As tens of thousands of Jews arrived in Palestine, the local Arab population feared that they would be forced out of their homeland, and riots broke out between the Jews and the Arabs.

After the Second World War, Jewish immigration increased and the situation worsened. British troops had to patrol the streets while diplomats tried to satisfy the demands of both groups. It was an impossible challenge. British forces pulled out of Palestine in 1948, leaving behind them a conflict that still rages today.

Mother country

Meanwhile, an old troopship called *Empire Windrush* was steaming across the Atlantic carrying passengers from Jamaica to Britain. As colonial subjects, many of them had fought for Britain in the war – alongside millions of men from the rest of the empire. Now, they were taking up the British government's invitation for people from the colonies to move to Britain and fill the jobs of workers who had died in the war. Immigrants later flowed in from the rest of the Caribbean, Africa and Asia too.

On the whole, the new arrivals were given a warm greeting. But immigrants still faced racial prejudice at work, in their choice of housing and in their everyday life.

Despite these torments, many of these post-war immigrants decided to stay. They and their families are now an integral part of British culture and society.

15

"The wind of change is blowing through this continent."

This is a line from a speech made by British Prime Minister Harold Macmillan, during a visit to Africa in 1960.

Three years earlier, the Gold Coast, now Ghana, had become the first British colony in Africa to gain independence.

By 1963, Nigeria, the Southern Cameroons, British Somaliland, Sierra Leone, Uganda, Kenya and Tanzania had all followed.

Immigrants wave from the decks of *Empire Windrush* as it arrives at London's Tilbury docks, June 22, 1948.

EMPIRE WINDRUSH

LONDON

Korean War

Cold War hostility turned into real conflict in 1950, when the North Korean army invaded South Korea.

The UN condemned the attack and thousands of British troops, including the future movie star Michael Caine, helped to defend South Korea in a war that lasted three years.

An official poster for the Festival of Britain

Festival time

In May 1951, King George VI opened a breathtaking display of modern architecture, art and design along the South Bank of the Thames, in London. The South Bank Exhibition was part of the Festival of Britain, a nationwide celebration organized by the government to mark the country's recovery from the dark days of the war. Millions of people flocked to the festival, confident that Britain was moving into better, brighter times.

Future shock

The festival had originally been planned to mark the centenary of the Great Exhibition of 1851, but it was clear to most visitors that the architects of the South Bank had their eyes set firmly on the future and not the past.

A striking, needle-shaped tower called the Skylon loomed over wide riverside walkways, and a giant Dome of Discovery boasted eight galleries portraying the natural world and Britain's contribution to science and exploration. The whole site set the style for projects that were taking shape around the country.

This photograph, taken in 1951, shows the site of London's South Bank Exhibition.

Radio beacon

Royal Festival Hall

A win for Winston

Clement Attlee believed the South Bank was a shining
example of the good work being done by his
government. But only months after the festival began,
the Labour Party was defeated in a general election and
Winston Churchill returned as Prime Minister. Tired
of putting the needs of the country before their own,
many voters were won over by Churchill's promises of
less state control and better living standards.

Churchill supported the National Health Service
and other successful Labour reforms, but he loathed
the architecture of the South Bank. When the festival
ended, he ordered most of the buildings to be
demolished. Only the walkways and a concert
auditorium – the Royal Festival Hall – survived.

On top of the world

In May 1953, two men from a British expedition
became the first to scale the world's tallest mountain
– Everest. Edmund Hillary, a New Zealander, and
Tenzing Norgay, from Nepal, were praised by
British journalists. But news of their
achievement had to share the headlines
with another historic celebration – the
coronation of a new queen, Elizabeth II.

Great Smog in the Big Smoke

Burning coal was the
main source of energy
in the early 1950s and
smog caused by smoke
was a problem in most
cities.

In December 1952,
thousands of people in
London died after thick
smog that lasted for
days. The air was so
filthy, people could
barely see in the streets.

The government
quickly brought in a
series of Clean Air acts
to reduce pollution.

The Skylon was dismantled
after the South Bank
Exhibition, but its site is
now home to Europe's
largest ferris wheel, the
London Eye.

Dome of Discovery   Skylon   County Hall

Elizabeth II greets her subjects from the balcony of Buckingham Palace, on the day of her coronation.

A crowning moment

The British monarchy was a source of pride for most people in the 1950s, setting an example of stability, duty and all that was best about the country. News of King George's sudden death at the age of 56 rocked the nation. After a year of mourning, the King's 25-year-old daughter, Elizabeth, was crowned at a lavish coronation in the summer of 1953. Although the ceremony followed centuries-old royal traditions, Queen Elizabeth II was determined to lead the monarchy into the modern age.

Ahead of the pack

In May, 1954, British sprinter Roger Bannister became the first man to run a mile in less than four minutes.

In the spotlight

The coronation was a breathtaking display of the royal family's wealth and international status. Crowds gathered to see Elizabeth journey to Westminster Abbey in a golden coach and political leaders from around the globe came to welcome the Queen as new head of the Commonwealth of Nations – a group of former British colonies. Against Churchill's advice, Elizabeth insisted that all her subjects should be able to witness the event. It was broadcast live on television, and around 20 million people tuned in to watch.

Shake, rattle and roll

While Queen Elizabeth embarked on a tour of the Commonwealth, Britain's young people and 'teenagers' – as the newspapers began to call them – were determined to have fun. They were starting to challenge the habits of their parents' generation and wanted new fashions and music to call their own. Gangs of 'Teddy Boys' borrowed a look from Edwardian times, and when an American movie, *Rock Around the Clock,* reached Britain in 1956, there were riots in cinemas as teenagers screamed and danced to the rock 'n' roll beats.

Shadow of the bomb

Meanwhile, Churchill struggled to arrange a peace summit between the leaders of America and the Soviet Union. By the mid-1950s, both countries had tested a complex and apocalyptic nuclear weapon – the hydrogen bomb. It was a thousand times more powerful than the atomic bombs dropped on Japan at the end of the Second World War.

Churchill feared the Cold War might flare into a world-destroying conflict but he still wanted Britain to be one of the 'Big Three' global superpowers. British scientists finally developed h-bomb technology after a series of tests on Christmas Island, in 1957.

Teen threads

Rock 'n' roll fans developed their own styles. Teddy Boys wore long, tailored jackets and suede shoes. Girls wore full skirts that billowed out as they jived to the music.

Power of protest

The protest group, CND – Campaign for Nuclear Disarmament – was launched in 1958 to press for a world without nuclear weapons.

A British designer, Gerald Holtom, provided the group's famous peace symbol, inspired by an image of a man holding out his hands in despair.

Some British spies found it hard to adjust to life as double agents in Moscow. Guy Burgess even asked friends back home to order him suits from his Savile Row tailor.

Sir Anthony Blunt was a respected art expert who had looked after the Queen's collection of paintings. But in 1979, he was exposed as one of the Cambridge spies. Blunt never stood trial but he lost his knighthood.

British Prime Minister Anthony Eden greets Soviet Communist Party leader, Nikita Khrushchev, outside 10 Downing Street, in 1956.

Spies, lies and Suez

Worn down by hard work and ill health, Churchill resigned as Prime Minister a few months after his 80th birthday. The man who took his place, the dashing Anthony Eden, met world leaders at the first post-war peace summit, held in Switzerland in 1955.

Soviet officials visited London the following year, amid signs that Cold War hostilities were beginning to thaw. But when Eden made a desperate military gamble in the Middle East, he took Britain nightmarishly close to a nuclear war.

Moscow exiles

Espionage and skulduggery flourished during the Cold War, as agents from both sides of the Iron Curtain tried to steal secrets and stay ahead in the spying game.

The British government was embarrassed when two of its former civil servants – Guy Burgess and Donald Maclean – were discovered living in Moscow. They belonged to a group of five spies from Cambridge University who had been acting as double agents, and passing secrets to the Soviets since the 1930s.

Mediterranean Sea

Beirut

SYRIA

LEBANON •Damascus

IRAQ

Baghdad•

The Suez Canal and the Middle East

ISRAEL

•Amman

Jerusalem •

Port Said

Suez Canal

JORDAN

SAUDI ARABIA

Cairo

EGYPT

Sinai Desert

Red Sea

River of oil

Because the region is rich in oilfields, the Middle East became a fiercely contested battleground in the Cold War. Britain kept troops there to guard the Suez Canal, a vital shipping route for oil from Iraq and cargoes from the east into the Mediterranean.

The canal was owned by Britain, France and other investors, who charged ships a fee to use it. But Egypt's President, Gamal Nasser, needed money to modernize his country. After persuading British troops to leave to area, he announced in July 1956 that the Suez Canal belonged to Egypt.

Cloak and dagger

Although Nasser offered to repay investors and allow ships from every country to use the canal, Eden was enraged. He told his ministers that he wanted Suez back in British hands and Nasser destroyed. American leaders and the Soviets warned him not to use military force, so Eden went to the UN to press his demands. But Nasser simply refused to give in. After months of fruitless diplomatic wrangling, the French government approached Eden with an astonishing secret plan to invade Egypt and reclaim the canal.

Getting angry

Upper-class characters dominated 1950s stage drama, but in 1956, John Osborne's play, *Look Back in Anger*, delivered a scathing attack on modern Britain from the lips of a working man.

The lead character, Jimmy Porter, rages against a nation obsessed with social class and the past glories of empire, and complains that there are "no good, brave causes" to fight for.

Journalists quickly linked Osborne with a group of writers who rejected pre-war values, nicknaming them the 'Angry Young Men'.

21

In this photograph you can see the tops of sunken ships blocking the entrance to the Suez Canal at Port Said. They were sunk on the orders of Egypt's President Nasser.

A lively debate

The writer and Angry Young Man, Kingsley Amis, had poked fun at the powers that be in his comic novel about university life, *Lucky Jim*.

Amis marched through Swansea to protest about Suez and was chased down the street by an angry woman who supported Eden.

Desert storm

The French scheme was so devious it was breathtaking. Israel was willing to attack Egypt's eastern borders in the Sinai Desert. With a war raging close to the canal, Britain and France could rush troops to the area and claim that they were there to protect the waterway. In all the commotion, the Soviets and the Americans would never guess that they had been tricked. Eden agreed to the plan and by the first week of November 1956, British commandos were storming across the beaches around Port Said.

Police or thieves?

Eden's decision to attack Egypt split the nation and sent shock waves around the world. The British public argued about the rights and wrongs of the invasion in their homes, in the street, in pubs and on the radio. Thousands marched in protest and several countries threatened to leave the Commonwealth, condemning Britain's action. But these were only minor problems for Eden when compared with the noises coming from the Soviet Union and the United States.

Caving in

In the opening days of the invasion, Soviet diplomats warned Eden that they had many allies in the Middle East and that they would, "crush the aggressors … and restore peace". If this wasn't bad enough, US President Dwight Eisenhower told Eden that America would freeze all financial aid to Britain until the country's troops left Egypt. Faced with the threat of Soviet missiles and economic disaster, Eden backed down. To the lasting fury of his French allies, he called an immediate ceasefire.

Bowing out

The pressures of what came to be known as the Suez Crisis ruined Anthony Eden's health. His doctors ordered him to rest, so he spent several weeks recuperating at 'Goldeneye' – the Jamaican home of the writer Ian Fleming. On his return to Britain, Eden soldiered on for a few more weeks, denying whispers about his pact with the French and refusing to accept that he had ever been in the wrong. He resigned early in 1957, passing the duties of Prime Minister to Harold Macmillan.

Britain lost more than a canal in the Suez Crisis. The events proved that the nation was no longer able to act alone on the international stage without American backing, and most people believed this marked the end of the country as a superpower. From then on, Britain had more in common with other European states than it did with the Soviet Union or the United States.

Agent 007

Ian Fleming's James Bond stories first appeared in 1953 with the publication of *Casino Royale*. Fleming wrote over a dozen Bond books at his Jamaican villa – some on a gold-plated typewriter.

After the success of the first Bond movie – *Dr. No* – Fleming's smooth-talking spy became a world-famous action hero who is still enormously popular today.

This is an illustration from a poster for the 1962 movie of *Dr. No*.

AS THE TREENS SWARM UP ASTERN, DAN FIRES THE OPENING SHOTS OF THE FIRST PITCHED BATTLE EVER FOUGHT IN SPACE.

Science fiction comics had been popular since the beginning of the 1950s. The most famous space hero was the square-jawed Dan Dare (shown above) who was constantly battling a baddy from Venus, called the Mekon.

Many designers were inspired by the geometric shapes and new materials used in the design of satellites and space rockets. During the 1950s and 60s, all kinds of household objects, from television sets and lampshades, to wallpaper and furniture, were given a 'futuristic' style.

Space Age

In the winter of 1957, Soviet scientists launched a small satellite – *Sputnik 1* – into orbit around the Earth. New technology was taking mankind into Space, and changing the way people lived.

In Britain, there were jobs for all. Families spent their newly acquired cash on cars, televisions and gadgets like toasters and washing machines, and they bought their groceries in new 'self-service' supermarkets that were appearing on the high streets.

The 'Space Age' was a boom time. Few would have argued with Prime Minister Harold Macmillan when he boasted, "most of our people have never had it so good."

Sight and sound

Millions of British households had invested in their first ever televisions to enjoy the coronation ceremony in 1953. At first, there was only one channel to watch – BBC. Then, in 1955, the independent television network, ITV, started beaming its shows, and adverts, to the nation.

Communications were improving too, although it was still rare for people to have telephones at home.

24

Nuclear stand-off

While images of the latest advances in Space technology fascinated television viewers in Britain and around the world, developments in weapons technology brought new fears. For two terrifying weeks in October 1962, all eyes and ears were glued to the news reports on television and radio, as a stand-off between the United States and the Soviet Union brought the world to the brink of a nuclear war.

On October 14, US spy planes spotted Soviet ships unloading missiles, and launch sites being built on the Caribbean island of Cuba, less than 100 miles from the coast of Florida. The US President, John F. Kennedy, threatened to invade Cuba if the missiles weren't removed, and to retaliate against the Soviet Union if any missiles were launched.

After tense negotiations, Soviet leader Nikita Khrushchev and President Kennedy came to an agreement, which was announced on October 28. The Cold War wasn't over yet, but the 'Cuban Missile Crisis' had been resolved, and the world breathed a sigh of relief.

In October, 1958, the BBC broadcast the very first episode of *Blue Peter*. Still watched by millions today, it's the longest-running children's television show ever.

The open road

In the late 1950s and early 60s, car sales in Britain rocketed.

In 1959, Britain's first motorway, the M1, was opened, and a new car, the Austin Mini, went on sale. The Mini quickly became a design icon. It was cheap, sleek and modern.

Many considered a Mini to be the ultimate fashion accessory.

This woman's Mini has been customized to match her dress.

The swinging sixties

The 1960s are often described as a special time in the story of Britain. During a decade that seemed louder, brighter and more eventful than any other since the war, British talent stormed the world stage, while Harold Wilson's Labour government promised to modernize the nation. But for all the glitter and noise of the sixties, change was slow across much of the country as people came to terms with new attitudes.

The Fab Four

Nobody did more to revolutionize modern music and make Britain hip than four young men from Liverpool – the Beatles. Formed in 1960, the band released a string of hits that started a teenage craze, 'Beatlemania', and quickly earned them international fame. Their long hair and cheeky confidence shocked older generations but the Beatles set the standard for future pop bands.

British pop artist, Peter Blake, designed an album cover for the Beatles. He arranged life-sized cutouts of famous people among stage props, and then photographed them.

The Beatles perform in bright stage costumes in 1967.

My generation

The Beatles were part of a new wave of British musicians, actors, photographers, artists and designers with one thing in common – they were all young. Bands like the Kinks, the Who and the Rolling Stones outraged parents of teenage fans with their wild concerts and wilder lifestyles. Social class seemed less important to success than in earlier decades and movie stars like Michael Caine and Sean Connery made no secret of their working-class roots.

Looking sharp

Searching for a fresh, unfussy look to match the times, designers produced simple, smart suits, A-shaped dresses and mini-skirts. They thought everyone should be able to afford the latest fashions.

While London's new 'boutique' shops were too expensive for most young people, the models and the photographers who made them famous were often from modest backgrounds. One of the most popular fashion and portrait photographers was David Bailey who had grown up in the East End of London.

King Harold

After 13 years of Conservative rule, Harold Wilson had won a narrow victory for Labour in 1964. He presented himself as an uncomplicated man of the people. But he was a brilliant, tactical politician who wanted to make Britain a fairer place, and planned to reform the country's industries and working habits. He faced an uphill struggle against massive national debts, millions of angry trades union members and a popular press that feared the country was heading for chaos.

Canvas to catwalk

The artist, Bridget Riley, was a pioneer of sixties Op Art – creating optical illusions in paint, with bold, black and white designs.

Fashion designers were inspired to produce Op Art mini-dresses. Riley thought this cheapened her work, but the dresses were very popular.

One of the leading fashion designers of the 1960s, and one of the first to introduce mini-dresses to the high street, was Mary Quant, shown here wearing one of her own designs.

Pickles the champ

In March 1966, the World Cup trophy was stolen. A dog named Pickles sniffed it out under a hedge in south London and his owner returned it in time for the final. Pickles became an instant celebrity, and won a year's supply of dog food.

Bobby Moore, captain of England's 1966 football team, holds aloft the World Cup trophy.

Gangster playboys

In the summer of 1963, a gang of crooks stopped a mail train and snatched millions of pounds. The Great Train Robbery fascinated the British public and journalists reported every detail of the pursuit, capture and trial of the gang members. One of the robbers, Ronnie Biggs, escaped from prison and lived as a fugitive in Brazil for decades. Some politicians complained that criminals were becoming stars, and protested when David Bailey included photographs of two London gangsters – the Kray twins – in a collection of celebrity portraits.

Champions

Newspaper editorials seethed about the decline in British moral standards, but a series of sporting triumphs in the mid-1960s gave them something to celebrate. For football fans, the 1966 World Cup was the stuff of legend. In a breathtaking final at Wembley Stadium, the English team battled cramp and fatigue to secure a 4-2 win over West Germany.

Campbell's *Bluebird-Proteus CN7*
reached the record-breaking speed
of 710 kmph (440 mph).

Breaking records

In 1964, Donald Campbell, a car and motor boat racer,
broke world speed records on both land and water.
Then in 1969, a British sailor, Robin Knox-Johnston,
won the Golden Globe Race, becoming the first solo
yachtsman to circle the globe without stopping.

Live and let live

Meanwhile, Harold Wilson's government
introduced a number of new laws, which had a
major impact on the way people lived. In 1965, the
death penalty for murder was abolished, and two years
later, abortion and male homosexuality became legal in
England and Wales. The courts also eased restrictions
on divorce, gambling and drinking alcohol.

Rivers of blood

Critics accused the government of encouraging a
more permissive society, but they saved their most
violent outbursts for the issue of immigration. In 1968,
a Conservative MP, Enoch Powell, made a speech
predicting bloodshed and disaster for Britain, unless the
flow of immigrants into the country was checked. Powell
was thrown out of the Conservative Party, but his views
were a stark reminder that a multi-racial, more
tolerant Britain was still a long way off.

Death of a statesman

In January 1965,
Winston Churchill died
at the age of 90. He was
given a spectacular
state funeral.

The coffin was
carried on a gun carriage
to St. Paul's Cathedral.
After the funeral service,
it sailed up the Thames on
a barge, with an RAF
fly-past.

From Waterloo,
it was taken by steam
train to Oxfordshire
where Churchill was
buried near his family
home, Blenheim Palace.

The science of life

Some of the most
exciting discoveries
of the 20th century
have been in the field
of genetics – the
study of
genes.

Genes exist
in every cell in
a person's body.
They contain
instructions that
affect how that person
looks and behaves –
from whether their
eyes are blue
or brown, to
whether they
are good at
Genes   sports.
are made up
of a chemical
called DNA.

This timeline shows
some of the scientific
discoveries that have
affected life in Britain
since the 1950s.

Many of the discoveries and inventions of the 20th
century were driven by the demands of war, but they
had a great impact on people's everyday lives, too.
Military research into rockets and jet planes helped
take astronauts to the moon, and the new materials first
developed for use in weapons and rockets – nylon,
hard plastics and synthetic rubber – were soon in
widespread use in people's homes.

Medical breakthroughs continued after the war too,
improving the prevention and treatment of many
diseases. The average life expectancy of someone born
in 1900 had been less than 50, partly because many
babies died in infancy, but by the end of the century,
most Britons could expect to live past 70.

However, some people believe medical research
has gone too far, and debates are still raging over
the possible risks of some innovations, such as
cloning and genetic modification of crops.

1950s

Scientists developed
contraceptive pills to
prevent pregnancy. The
pills became available to the
public in the 1960s.

1967

In South Africa, Dr. Christiaan Barnard
carried out the first successful heart
transplant. The following year, the procedure
was performed in Britain for the first time.

1950s

Rosalind Franklin took
the first photographs
of DNA, helping Francis
Crick and James Watson
to make breakthroughs in
understanding its structure.

1954

Doctors successfully tested a
vaccine for polio – an infectious
disease which attacks muscles
and can be fatal.

1970s

Medical lasers were used instead of scalpels for the first time in eye surgery.

1970s

A vaccine was developed to protect people from measles, mumps and rubella (MMR) with a single injection. It was introduced in Britain in 1988.

1978

The world's first 'test-tube baby', Louise Brown, was born in Manchester. She was conceived in a laboratory instead of inside her mother's body.

1981

A new disease, AIDS, was reported and later found to be caused by a virus known as HIV. One of the first people in Britain to die with AIDS was Terrence Higgins, in July 1983. A charity set up in his name has been at the forefront of the fight against HIV and AIDS ever since.

Wearing a red ribbon shows support for people affected by AIDS.

1990s

Scientists began to produce the first food crops that were genetically modified (GM) to make them grow bigger or more resistant to diseases.

1990s

Thousands of British cattle became infected with BSE, or 'mad cow disease', which can spread to humans, through beef. Millions of cows were destroyed to try to stamp out the disease.

1997

Scientists used DNA from one sheep to grow, or 'clone' another identical sheep, which they called Dolly.

Fragile Earth

Since the 1970s, people have become increasingly worried about the damage that humans cause to the environment.

Deforestation is driving many species to extinction.

Some substances, such as the gases in aerosol cans, damage the ozone layer, a layer of protective gases that surrounds the Earth.

Burning fossil fuels, such as coal and oil, causes global warming. This is a slow rise in air temperature which could have a serious impact on the world's climate.

A schoolgirl does her homework by candlelight during a power cut in February 1972.

Blackout

By the late 1960s, millions of British workers belonged to trades union groups that had formed to protect their working rights and living standards. But many British industries were sluggish and outdated, and the pound had lost value against foreign currencies, making imported fuel, food and goods expensive. With prices rising, workers demanded higher wages, and the unions called walkouts, or strikes, if these were refused.

Sonic zoom

The faster-than-sound passenger jet, Concorde, made its maiden flight in 1969. It could cross the Atlantic in under three hours and was the pride of the British air fleet until its last flights in 2003.

Promises, promises

In 1970, the Conservative Party came into power promising, "a better tomorrow" with fewer strikes or price increases. But the new Prime Minister, Edward Heath, was soon battling strikes by dockworkers and postmen. In 1972, the miners went on strike over pay and asked other workers not to move coal to power stations. Homes across the country suffered electricity cuts, schools and offices closed, and MPs in the House of Commons held meetings by the light of oil lanterns. Heath quickly caved in to the miners' demands.

Trading places

Away from the turmoil of striking unions, Heath pushed for Britain to join the European Economic Community, also known as the Common Market. For years, the French government had blocked British attempts to join this alliance of trading nations, and some diplomats believed it was because they were still angry about Suez.

Britain finally became a full member of the EEC in 1973. Close partnership with Europe has been a vital contribution to the growth of the nation ever since.

New money

In 1971 the Bank of England introduced a decimal system of 100 pence to a pound. It issued new coins to replace the old currency of 12 pence to a shilling and 20 shillings to a pound.

Can't pay, won't pay

When the miners' union leader, Arthur Scargill, threatened another strike, Heath ordered companies to save energy by reducing their working hours. With millions of people working a three-day week and more power cuts looming, Heath called an election in 1974 and asked voters to decide who was running the country – the unions or the government. He lost, and when Harold Wilson returned to 10 Downing Street the miners got their money.

These miners' wives are out in support of their husbands' strike for better wages.

Bloody Sunday

When British rule ended in Ireland in the 1920s, fighting broke out between Catholics and Protestants in the north of the country. The Protestant majority there refused to join the Irish Free State and, after fifty years of violence and feuding, Northern Ireland was still part of the United Kingdom.

Members of an armed group, the IRA – Irish Republican Army – had been struggling for decades to turn Ireland into one country. But by the late 1960s, they were losing support.

Street fighters

The region was blighted by unemployment and poverty, and many Catholics thought they were treated like second-class citizens. From 1967, Catholic groups started organizing marches and peaceful demonstrations to demand jobs and better housing. But Protestant groups began counter-demonstrations, and violence flared up between them. Police tried to block the marches and disperse the crowds. Meanwhile, IRA gunmen set up barricades and military-style checkpoints on street corners.

Wall art

On the streets of Northern Ireland, many houses have been painted with murals that show support for different sides in the dispute.

The IRA mural shown above is titled 'The Easter Rising' in Gaelic. This was an unsuccessful rising against British rule, that took place in Dublin in 1916.

Police officers, armed with riot shields and batons, face rioters in Bogside, Londonderry, in 1969.

The Battle of Bogside

In August 1969, after three days of fierce riots in the Bogside area of Londonderry, local police appealed to the British army for help. Soldiers ringed the area, but made no attempt to fight their way in.

For more than a year, the Bogside was a tense, no-go zone for the authorities. Then, one Sunday, January 30, 1972, thousands of Catholics gathered for another march, and army commanders brought in a force of paratrooper combat soldiers.

Road to ruin

When some youths following the march began to throw stones, the paratroopers rushed in to arrest them. In the confusion of the riot, the paratroopers thought they were under attack from IRA snipers and started shooting. Within minutes they had killed 13 people and injured over a dozen more.

None of those who were shot had been carrying guns, and people around the world were quick to call it a massacre. Fury over the 'Bloody Sunday' shootings swelled the ranks of the IRA and sparked years of vicious fighting that are known as the Troubles.

Breaking away

Northern Ireland wasn't the only part of the UK to feel let down by politicians in London.

Communities in Wales and Scotland were hit hard by job losses and a lack of investment by the government.

In the 1970s, they stepped up their own campaigns for more power over local issues.

The Welsh Language Society battled to protect the cultural traditions of Wales, while the Scottish National Party attracted voters with the promise of independence.

God save the Queen

In the late 1970s, more and more workers went on strike demanding better pay and conditions. But, in spite of the gloomy news, people made a special effort to celebrate the Queen's Silver Jubilee in 1977, marking 25 years since Elizabeth II had come to the throne.

A royal salute

Queen Elizabeth toured the Commonwealth and the British Isles in her Jubilee year, greeting vast crowds in many cities. On June 7, over a million people lined her route through London to a thanksgiving ceremony attended by world leaders including US President, Jimmy Carter.

Local communities organized street parties for children across the land, decking their houses with flags, bunting and portraits of the royal family.

The government gave millions of British children Jubilee gifts – including commemorative mugs.

Queen Elizabeth meets some enthusiastic subjects during her Jubilee tour of Britain.

Smash it up

The Queen was popular with the wartime generation, but after the social changes and economic havoc of the 1960s and 70s, some young people didn't feel proud of Britain or loyal to institutions like the monarchy.

A new style of rock music called 'punk' voiced their anger and contempt for authority. Punks dressed in torn clothes and dyed their hair. They set out to shock their parents, politicians and the police.

Punk band the Sex Pistols' anthem, *God Save the Queen*, mocked the royal family and hit the top of the charts in Jubilee week.

Crisis? What crisis?

In January 1979, amid strikes by transport workers, the Labour Prime Minister, James Callaghan, snapped at reporters when they suggested there was mounting chaos across the country. In what became known as the 'winter of discontent', truck drivers, waste collectors and even gravediggers joined the strike, demanding more pay. Mountains of uncollected rubbish rotted in the streets and soldiers stood in for striking firemen and ambulance drivers.

The outrageous fashion designer Vivienne Westwood, posing below in red tartan, helped to define the punk style.

Maggie steps in

Callaghan had replaced Harold Wilson in 1976. He had a calm, reassuring style of leadership but he underestimated the sense of panic that was gripping the nation. In May 1979, Callaghan was forced to hold a general election. Campaigning under the slogan "Labour isn't working", the winner was the first woman to be Prime Minister – Margaret Thatcher.

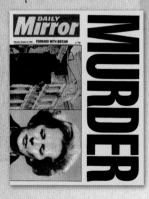

Battlefield Britain

Fresh from her election victory, Margaret Thatcher greeted journalists with a quote from St. Francis of Assisi: "Where there is discord, may we bring harmony". But for all Thatcher's promises to unite the country, Britain seemed more divided than ever.

Only weeks earlier, members of a racist group – the National Front – had been on the rampage in London. The IRA was killing British soldiers and civilians, and people in poor city suburbs were angry and ready to riot.

A woman's touch

Thatcher's parents were shopkeepers and she was brought up to believe in hard work and standing on your own two feet. She won a scholarship to Oxford University to study Chemistry before going into politics. Thatcher scorned Attlee's vision of cradle-to-grave state care, she took a hard line on immigration and spoke of the national character being "swamped" if too many immigrants were allowed into the UK.

An overturned car burns as a police van arrives in Brixton during the riots of 1981.

Making a stand

In April 1979, the National Front held a rally at Southall Town Hall in London. Immigrants from India had put down roots in Southall but the National Front wanted them to leave the country. Thousands of residents and anti-racist demonstrators gathered to stop the meeting and one of them, a teacher named Blair Peach, died during a charge by riot police.

Riots broke out in the London suburb of Brixton in the summer of 1981, after people from the local Afro-Caribbean community accused the police of being aggressive and racist. Rioters burned cars and buildings, looted shops and hurled bricks at the police – scenes that would be repeated in Brixton and other city suburbs before the end of the decade.

Despite these tensions, National Front membership collapsed in the 1980s and Southall's Blair Peach Primary School is a thriving, multi-racial success to this day.

Wedding of the century

On July 29, 1981, Prince Charles, the heir to the throne, and Lady Diana Spencer were married in St. Paul's Cathedral in front of 3,500 guests and some 750 million television viewers around the globe.

Against the backdrop of street violence and economic misery, the wedding provided many Britons with some much-needed fairytale romance. Sadly, the marriage was not to last.

Dinner lady

Margaret Thatcher had battled prejudice to win the top job in British politics but her support for traditional family values made her unpopular with many women fighting for change.

According to Margaret Thatcher's son, "she used to come home from Westminster and immediately start cooking the dinner."

Writing on the wall

Many women were offended by the sexist language and images that were often used in advertisements. Some took matters into their own hands, defacing posters and painting their own slogans until advertisers were forced to change.

Women on the march

In the early 20th century, job prospects for women were far more limited than they were for men. The war years gave many young women their first taste of independence as they took up the jobs of men sent overseas with the armed forces.

When peace came, most men expected women to stop work and accept a life as mothers and homemakers. But from the 1960s, women in Britain and around the world started a revolution to smash old attitudes and win the same rights and opportunities as men.

No job for a lady

Paid employment gave women more control and choice over how to live, but they usually earned less than men doing the same job. In 1968, female car workers in London went on strike, demanding equal pay.

Strikes across Britain forced the government to pass an Equal Pay Act in 1970 and further laws provided maternity rights and nursery care for the children of working women. Even with these changes, women today are still under-represented in many professions and are often paid less than men.

More than a pretty face

After the war, the British media and entertainment industry was still dominated by men, and lots of women objected to the way they were portrayed as cute, unthinking objects on television and in books, magazines and advertisements. In 1970, women protesters stormed into a London beauty competition, blowing whistles and pelting the tuxedoed host, Bob Hope, with flour bombs until he ran from the stage.

40

Tearing down the fence

In 1981, when the British government agreed to store American nuclear missiles at an RAF base at Greenham Common in southern England, a small group of women marched from Wales to raise their concerns about the threat of nuclear war. They set up a peace camp along the perimeter fence of the base. By the following year, tens of thousands of women were flooding to the camp to join the protest.

Mothers, daughters, sisters and wives journeyed from all corners of Britain to make their voices heard. Most stayed for a day or two, helping around the camp, blocking military vehicles and linking hands in a plea for peace that caught the attention of the world.

The missiles were finally removed from Greenham Common in 1991, but the women's peace camp remained until September 2000.

During their 'Embrace the Base' protest at Greenham Common in 1982, women linked hands all the way around the perimeter fence.

Protesters decorated the fence with banners and things of personal significance, including clothes, toys, family photographs and poems.

A selection of button badges worn by the protesters

The Iron Lady

After three years in power, Margaret Thatcher had made herself very unpopular. Many of her Conservative colleagues disagreed with her ideas about how to revive the economy, but she insisted she was right, declaring, "you turn if you want to. The lady's not for turning." Despite her confidence, unemployment and poverty were rising.

With a general election due in 1983, it looked as though Thatcher's days at the top were almost over – unless she could win over Britain's voters. Then in April 1982, she got the chance to do just that.

"I am extraordinarily patient, provided I get my own way in the end."

Margaret Thatcher

A distant war

The Falkland Islands, off the coast of Argentina, were among the last remaining British colonies. But the Argentinians had always claimed that the islands belonged to them. On April 2, they invaded without warning, and the islanders appealed to Britain for help.

The empire strikes back

Thatcher had won the nickname 'the Iron Lady' because of her strong leadership. Now she lived up to that reputation, and sent a force by sea to retake the islands. The Falklands War had begun.

Thatcher was taking a big gamble. Many people feared that the war would end in a humiliating withdrawal, just like the Suez Crisis. But although the UN condemned Britain for going to war, they did not intervene. Within 73 days, British forces had recaptured the islands, and the Argentinians had to surrender.

Thatcher's gamble had paid off. Her supporters called her a national hero, and she won a resounding victory in the 1983 general election.

This is the Sun newspaper's front page, after a British submarine sank an Argentinian ship, *General Belgrano*. More than 300 Argentinians had been killed, and many British people were horrified by the heartless headline.

In Portsmouth, crowds welcome home HMS *Invincible*, back from fighting in the Falklands War.

Greed is good

Margaret Thatcher had big plans for Britain. She wanted to reduce the role of government in people's lives, encouraging them to fend for themselves.

Her style of politics – Thatcherism – transformed the country, but critics accused her of splitting the nation into haves and have-nots. The rich grew richer but millions of workers lost their jobs and had to claim unemployment benefit, or 'dole' money, in order to survive.

This puppet of Thatcher was made for the satirical television show, *Spitting Image*, which used puppets to poke fun at politicians and celebrities through the 80s and early 90s.

Black gold

During the 1960s, geologists discovered vast oil fields off the coast of Shetland and northern Scotland. Queen Elizabeth opened the first oil pipeline to the mainland in 1975. Storms and heavy seas in this wild region have cost the lives of dozens of workers, but North Sea oil has been a vital source of wealth and fuel for the nation ever since.

Home sweet home

Thatcher wanted as many people as possible to have the chance to own their house, so she brought in a 'right to buy' scheme. This enabled tenants who rented council houses to buy them cheaply.

Hundreds of thousands of people became homeowners for the first time in their lives. But the scheme meant that rented council housing remained only in the poorest areas. Many of those who couldn't buy were isolated in crumbling tower blocks.

Selling the silver

Meanwhile, Thatcher began a process of 'privatization' – selling off the big industries that Clement Attlee had nationalized. She thought they would be more efficient if they were run by private companies again, instead of by the government.

Labour politicians hated this idea, and even the former Conservative leader Harold Macmillan disapproved – he said it was like selling off the family silver. Without the government's support, some of these industries went bankrupt. But over time, others became more profitable.

Money, money, money

The changes didn't stop there. The government abolished controls on British banks that had been in place since the Second World War. Some banks collapsed, but others became vastly more successful, as they were now free to do more business overseas.

Not everyone agreed with Thatcher's policies, but the economy was improving. Thatcher wanted people to be free to make as much money as possible, and encouraged entrepreneurs to start up new businesses. It was easier to borrow money than before, and there was a spending frenzy.

Wealthy 'yuppies' (young urban professionals) showed off by driving gleaming sports cars, dining at expensive restaurants and taking extravagant holidays abroad. They were having the time of their lives.

On the go

In 1979, Sony produced the Walkman®, the world's first personal music player. It was very popular in Britain.

Meanwhile, businessmen were using mobile phones for the first time. They were huge and heavy by today's standards.

Traders in part of London's stock exchange compete to get the best deals. Their jackets show what their role is or which company they represent.

Miners who carried on working during strikes were called 'scabs'. They were often threatened or attacked by the strikers, so police were called in to protect them.

Everybody out

The miners' union set up 'picket lines' of strikers at the gates of mines to stop other miners from going to work. It even sent coachloads of strikers – 'flying pickets' – to blockade any pits that were still working.

Coal not dole

Not everyone did so well out of Thatcher's policies. In 1984, she tried to close down 20 coal mines, because she was convinced that they were unprofitable. Thousands stood to lose their jobs, and entire mining communities were threatened with poverty. Miners across the nation went on a mass strike, hoping to force the Prime Minister to change her mind.

Thatcher had given in to striking miners three years earlier, but this time, the Iron Lady stood her ground. The government had stored up coal and oil in advance, so that the nation's power supply wouldn't be cut off by the lack of coal.

It was the longest strike in British history, dragging on for a whole year, with violent confrontations between police and strikers. But eventually, the miners couldn't afford to continue the strike any longer. The mines were closed. Thatcher had won.

Broken cities

Coal miners weren't the only ones to suffer under Thatcher's government. Thousands of workers in the industries weakened by privatization lost their jobs, in steel plants, shipyards and factory assembly lines. The government also changed the rates of tax, collecting less from high earners and taking more from the poor. This rewarded successful business owners and professionals but it made life harder for people on low wages.

Industrial cities in the north of England, Wales and Scotland were hit the hardest. Here, unemployment led to poverty, homelessness and crime. While London bankers sipped champagne, growing numbers of homeless people were sleeping rough on city streets.

Sound of the underground

Many young people, especially in industrial cities, were jobless with few prospects. Some took out their frustrations on the football terraces, going to matches to fight fans of rival teams. Others turned to 'acid house' – dance music from the US, with a heavy, repetitive beat.

Dance parties, or 'raves', took place in clubs, abandoned industrial buildings and out in the countryside. Many of these were illegal, involving hundreds of guests and widespread drug use. Ravers left their worries behind and danced all night – many didn't have a job to go to the next morning.

The authorities weren't happy about these gatherings. But as murmurs of discontent grew louder, the Prime Minister had far bigger things to worry about.

Ravers dance to
acid house music.

Foreign crazes

During the 1980s, many trends from overseas took hold in Britain.

In 1980, the Rubik's Cube® arrived. Invented by a Hungarian architect, this deceptively simple puzzle became one of the most popular toys of all time.

Skateboards and BMX bikes became common in British streets. Both came from the US.

In the mid 1980s, there was a craze for breakdancing. It came from New York, where dancers performed amazing gymnastic feats to hip-hop music.

The Band Aid single topped the British charts for five weeks over Christmas in 1984-5. The record sold over three million copies, raising money to help relieve the famine in Ethiopia.

An audience of over 72,000 packed Wembley Stadium in London to watch the Live Aid concert.

One world

The 1980s were hard years for many British families, rocked by city riots, job cuts and brutal politics. But, in the summer of 1985, all that was put into a new perspective as people looked to Ethiopia, where a nation was starving after years of drought and failed crops. Two musicians had an ambitious idea to raise money and for a few hours it looked as though people really could join together to change the world.

The global jukebox

Bob Geldof and Midge Ure first asked their pop star friends and contacts to sing on a charity record after seeing news reports of the famine in 1984. The Band Aid record sold a million copies in a week and Geldof and Ure decided to stage a concert – Live Aid – featuring the biggest names in music at that time.

On July 13, 1985, dozens of stars played at Wembley Stadium and in cities around the world. The public donated over 150 million pounds; about 1.5 billion people saw the show live on television and Geldof won a knighthood.

A worldwide disease

The rock band Queen stole the show at Live Aid, with an amazing performance by their lead singer, Freddie Mercury. But only six years after his triumph at Wembley, Mercury was dead, killed by a terrifying disease that was spreading quickly around the world. AIDS attacks the immune system of its victims, making them vulnerable to infection and disease.

Scientists developed drugs to fight the virus that causes AIDS in the 1990s, but millions of people with no access to proper medical care are still dying with the illness today. People and gather on World AIDS Day – December 1 – to show their support for sufferers, to mourn lost friends and to raise funds to fight the disease.

Prince Charles and Princess Diana officially opened the Live Aid concert at Wembley. After that, Diana became increasingly involved in charity work, especially for sufferers of AIDS and children affected by poverty and war.

Computers changed a lot during the 20th century, becoming smaller and cheaper.

The first electronic computers, built during the Second World War, filled up whole rooms. They were used for military purposes, such as breaking codes.

In the late 1970s, the first home computers were launched, and computer games soon became very popular. They were very basic by today's standards.

People who couldn't afford a home computer could play the games in video arcades.

Mutiny

On October 19, 1987 – 'Black Monday' – the economic boom came to an abrupt end. In Britain and around the world, stock markets crashed and the banks lost a lot of money. Undaunted, Thatcher pushed ahead with a number of ambitious and unpopular reforms, including a disastrous plan to change the tax system.

Tax rebels

In 1989, the government introduced the Community Charge – a new tax to pay for services provided by local councils. Apart from the unemployed and those on very low wages, all adults had to pay a fixed rate, whether they lived in a stately home or a bedsit.

Almost everyone thought this was unfair, and began calling it the Poll Tax, after the tax which had caused the Peasants' Revolt in the Middle Ages. Thousands refused to pay, and there were riots in the streets. Thatcher had no choice but to back down.

Protesters clash with police in London's Trafalgar Square, during the Poll Tax riots of March 1990.

Maggie out

The Prime Minister had few allies left in her
government, and in November 1990, she was
challenged for leadership of the party. Eventually, she
accepted that she would lose, and so, after eleven
turbulent years, the Iron Lady finally stood down.

It was her Chancellor, John Major, who stepped into
the breach. He was a quiet, calm man, and many
people were surprised that he had won the leadership.

Poll position

When a general election was called in April 1992,
most opinion polls predicted a win for the Labour
Party, led by Neil Kinnock. But on the morning of
the election, the Sun newspaper ran the headline,
"If Kinnock wins today will the last person to
leave Britain please turn out the lights." The
Sun's campaign may have swung the vote – the
Conservatives were victorious once again.

A Major success

John Major had an
unusual background. His
father had been a circus
performer, and later
ran a business
selling garden
gnomes.

Before going
into politics, John
Major worked as a
banker. The joke went
that he was the first
person to run away
from the circus to
join a bank.

The Iron Curtain lifts

In 1985, Mikhael Gorbachev became leader of the Soviet Union.

The Cold War began to thaw as Gorbachev reformed the Soviet Union and formed good relationships with other world leaders, including Margaret Thatcher.

At the end of the 80s, the Soviet Union collapsed, and the Berlin Wall was pulled down. A symbol of the Cold War, it had split the city into Communist East and non-Communist West since 1961.

Battle stations

In 1990, pictures taken by UN spy satellites revealed that President Saddam Hussein of Iraq was gathering troops to attack nearby Kuwait. On August 2, the Iraqis invaded.

The UN issued Saddam Hussein with an ultimatum: withdraw by January 15 the next year, or UN forces would drive the Iraqis out. Sadam refused, and so, on January 17, British troops went to war as part of the UN's mission, Operation Desert Storm.

A storm in the desert

The mission began with a heavy bombing campaign. Then came the ground assault, led by the crack troops of the British SAS (Special Air Service). Within days, the Iraqis were retreating. They burned Kuwaiti oil wells as they went, lighting up the desert with bursts of flame and sending clouds of acrid smoke into the sky.

The war was over in less than a month, and was a decisive victory for the UN forces. But Saddam Hussein remained in power, and Kuwait's economy was hit hard by the destruction of its oil wells.

This photograph shows a British tank crew in action in Kuwait. They are from the 7th Armoured Brigade, nicknamed 'Desert Rats'.

International police

As a member of both the UN and NATO, Britain sent troops to help in several other peacekeeping operations during the 90s. Many of these missions took place in the Balkans in eastern Europe, where chaos and civil war broke out among many communities as the Cold War came to an end.

British or European?

While British soldiers fought alongside Germans, French and Italians, British politicians were working with their continental counterparts, too.

In 1992, John Major signed the Maastricht Treaty, which reformed the EEC into the European Union. The EU was a political union with its own laws and policies. Some people were pleased that Britain was becoming more closely connected to the rest of Europe, while others feared that the country might lose its independence.

Royals in crisis

In a speech made on November 24, 1992, at an event marking her 40th anniversary on the throne, Queen Elizabeth described the year as an *"annus horribilis"* – which means "horrible year" in Latin.

Earlier in the year, it had been announced that her son, Prince Andrew, would separate from his wife, and his sister, Princess Anne, divorced her husband.

In November, there was a huge fire at Windsor Castle, which caused £40 million worth of damage.

Finally, in December, it was announced that Prince Charles and Diana would separate.

New Labour

In 1994, desperate to improve their fortunes after four election defeats, Labour Party members chose a new leader with a bold vision for Britain: Tony Blair. He believed that the only way to win power was to reform – and rebrand – the party.

Under Blair, 'New Labour', as he called it, dropped one of the party's oldest beliefs, that the country's big industries should be nationalized. Instead, Blair promised to spend more money on the NHS and education, while keeping taxes low to let business groups and individuals enjoy the money they earned.

In a series of dazzling speeches, Blair set out his plan to build a caring and prosperous society in modern Britain.

Closer to Europe

In 1994, the Channel Tunnel opened, linking Britain to France.

A joint project between the two nations, it had taken seven years to complete, and was referred to by some as one of the seven wonders of the modern world.

Tony Blair greets his supporters after winning the 1997 election.

A vote for change

While Blair's star was rising, John Major's government was becoming increasingly unpopular. On 'Black Wednesday' – September 16, 1992 – the pound had plummeted in value, forcing Major to change his economic policies. To make things worse, there were several scandals involving important Conservative politicians.

In May 1997, a general election was held, and the Labour Party swept to power promising that, "things can only get better."

At 43, Blair became the youngest Prime Minister of the 20th century. Many people saw his leadership as a breath of fresh air after 18 years of Conservative government.

Princess Diana died in a car
crash in August 1997. Here, Prince
Charles and his sons, William and Harry, survey
the flowers left outside her home at Kensington Palace.

Speaking for the nation

Tony Blair promised to give people from all
backgrounds a voice in politics, and wanted his
government to reflect better the diversity of the
population it represented. With his election victory,
five Asian and four African-British MPs were elected,
and the number of female MPs doubled to 120.

On August 31, Princess Diana was killed in a car
crash in Paris. Her death caused a tide of public
mourning, and when Queen Elizabeth kept silent,
many accused her of being cold and unfeeling. Blair,
on the other hand, understood the British public's
love for Diana and found the words to salute
her. In a hastily prepared statement, he called
her the "people's princess" and showed he was
a man in touch with the mood of the nation.

Goodbye, Hong Kong

At midnight on July 1,
1997, the British handed
over their last great
colony, Hong Kong, to
China. The British flag
was lowered, and the
Chinese flag was
raised in
its place.

Flying the flag

While Tony Blair was winning fame around the world, Britain enjoyed a boom in homegrown talent. Journalists were quick to claim that London was as 'swinging' as it had been in the 1960s, and a wave of artists, musicians and writers celebrated life in 'Cool Britannia'. After years in the doldrums, it was suddenly fashionable for British stars to wave the Union Jack.

Spice it up

Rejecting the American music that had been popular throughout the 1980s, British bands in the early 1990s started to write songs about their own everyday experiences and what it was like to be growing up in modern Britain. Britpop acts like Oasis and Blur were influenced by the musical legacy of the Beatles and the Kinks, and they sold millions of records.

Instead of defacing and lampooning the symbols of the nation – as the Punks had done – Britpop musicians put Union Jack images on guitars and album covers and seemed proud of their roots.

Hip or hyped?

During his first months in office, Blair was eager to promote the idea of 'Cool Britannia', so he invited rock stars and celebrities to meet him, causing some people to wonder whether he was more interested in publicity than politics.

Geri Halliwell - singer with the 90s pop band, the Spice Girls - caused quite a stir when she performed in her Union Jack mini-dress.

The Physical Impossibility of Death in the Mind of Someone Living, by Young British Artist Damien Hirst, is a real dead shark suspended in formaldehyde to stop the body from decaying.

Art with bite

By the mid-1990s, artworks made by a group nicknamed the Young British Artists were stealing the limelight at galleries around the world.

Many of the YBAs had moved away from painting to make large installations – clusters of objects, images and even movie clips arranged in glass boxes or gallery rooms. They encouraged viewers to look at familiar things in a new light, and their work had an instant appeal that brought millions of young people into galleries and made international stars of the artists.

Digital horizons

It was a British engineer – Tim Berners-Lee – who first imagined a 'world wide web' of linked computers sharing information. In 1990, he helped design a computer code for programmers and users who wanted to read and create websites. Using this as a common language between machines, the internet exploded into life, and gave birth to a new form of communication – email.

The internet has transformed industries and changed the way people shop, travel and interact. Thanks to the internet, we can now share photos, music and messages instantly with people all around the world.

Another Young British Artist, Tracey Emin, caused controversy when she included her own unmade bed in an exhibition.

Critics questioned whether this was really art, and a group of Japanese performance artists staged pillow fight on the bed in protest.

To rebuild Britain's public services, Blair's minister in charge of economic policy, Gordon Brown, came up with a controversial scheme to let private companies construct hundreds of schools and hospitals in return for long rental contracts with the government.

Meanwhile, billions of pounds from National Lottery ticket sales went into transforming Britain's sports and cultural institutions and helped to finance some dazzling works of art.

A new Jerusalem

After a year in office, Tony Blair was struggling to deliver on his election promises. Critics accused him of being a lightweight charmer who could never match the revolutionary achievements of Attlee's government.

As the end of the millennium drew near, Attlee's dream of building 'a new Jerusalem' still seemed a long way off. But many aspects of life in Britain had improved since the war. Many people could afford new homes, cars and holidays. And, at last, there was a chance for peace in Northern Ireland.

Building bridges

On Good Friday, April 10, 1998, the rival groups who had fought for control of Northern Ireland for almost 30 years agreed to destroy their weapons and join an elected assembly – or government – to decide the future of the region.

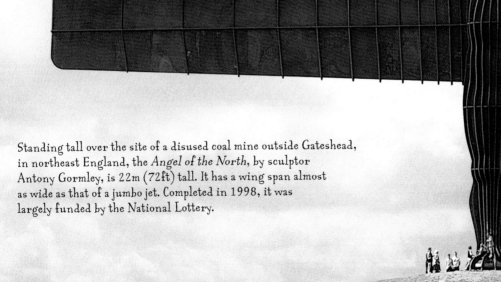

Standing tall over the site of a disused coal mine outside Gateshead, in northeast England, the *Angel of the North*, by sculptor Antony Gormley, is 22m (72ft) tall. It has a wing span almost as wide as that of a jumbo jet. Completed in 1998, it was largely funded by the National Lottery.

Dozens of people had helped to shape the Good Friday Agreement, but Tony Blair and the Irish Prime Minister, Bertie Ahern, both played a vital part in the negotiations. Unrest still occasionally flares up, but most Irish people are determined to protect the peace and never return to the horror of the Troubles.

Sharing the power

Tony Blair wanted to make Britain more democratic. In 1999, the Welsh Assembly and the Scottish Parliament were created, and powers over local decisions were transferred from Parliament in London to these elected regional assemblies. This process is known as devolution.

Blair also brought in new rules about how political parties were funded, as well as making plans for an elected Mayor of London, and to reform the House of Lords.

Lords and Ladies

Parliament in London is made up of the House of Commons and the House of Lords. Members of the House of Lords, known as Peers, help to make new laws.

In 1999, Blair removed the voting rights of Peers who had inherited their positions, rather than being elected.

Using an idea from the Ancient Greeks, Blair invited ordinary voters to serve as 'People's Peers'.

Thousands volunteered, from teachers to lollipop ladies, but the 15 men and women chosen were mostly senior figures from universities, branches of government or the business world.

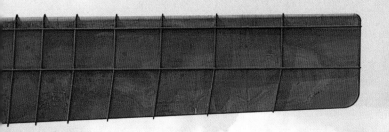

"The wings ... are not flat, they're about 3.5 degrees forward and give a sense of embrace."

Antony Gormley describes the *Angel of the North*.

Millennium buildings

Monuments were built all over Britain to mark the millennium.

The Gateshead Bridge in Newcastle spans the River Tyne. It can tilt to allow ships to pass underneath.

The Glasgow Science Centre stands beside the River Clyde. Its smooth, shiny surface is coated with titanium plates.

The Millennium Dome is a vast arena on the banks of the Thames in London. It is the biggest dome in the world.

Millennium

As the clock ticked down to midnight on December 31, 1999, the people of Britain celebrated the end of a century, and the dawn of a new millennium. Some people stayed at home with their families, while others held parties, or gathered in city streets to see in the New Year. At the stroke of twelve, Big Ben began to toll, as cheers went up and rockets were launched into the night sky.

Wrapped up warm against the chilly night, the people of Britain gazed up at fireworks bursting high above them. The 20th century had brought two world wars, the loss of an empire, and more rapid changes in science, culture and medicine than ever before. But who could say what challenges the new millennium would bring?

In London, crowds line the banks of the Thames and Westminster Bridge, to watch the New Year fireworks display.

Index

Acknowledgements

Every effort has been made to trace and acknowledge ownership of copyright. If any rights have been omitted, the publishers offer to rectify this in any future editions following notification. The publishers are grateful to the following individuals and organizations for their permission to reproduce material on the following pages: (t=top, b=bottom, l=left, r=right, m=middle)

cover (t) © Antony Nettle/Alamy, **(m)** © Getty Image/Hulton Archive/Bill Brandt; **p1** © Getty Images; p2-3 © Graeme Peacock/Alamy; **p6** © Popperfoto/Getty Images; **p7 (tr)** © Museum of London, **(br)** © Hulton-Deutsch Collection/CORBIS; **p9** © Bettmann/CORBIS; **p10** ©1999 Topham Picturepoint TopFoto.co.uk; **p11** © Mary Evans Picture Library; **p12** IOC/Olympic Museum Collections; **p13** © Bettmann/CORBIS; **p14** © The Estate of Henry Eveleigh/ Private Collection/Archives Charmet/The Bridgeman Art Library; **p15** © Getty Images; **p16-17** © Mary Evans Picture Library/Alamy; **p16 (l)** The National Archives UK DN7525; **p18** © Fox Photos/Hulton Archive/Getty Images; **p20** © Time & Life Pictures/Getty Images; **p22** © Getty Images; **p23** © Everett Collection/Rex Features; **p24** © Reproduced by kind permission of the Dan Dare Corporation Limited; **p25** © Trinity Mirror/Mirrorpix/Alamy; **p26-27** (background) © Jim Grant/Photodisc/Getty Images; **p26** © Everett Collection/Rex Features; **p27** © Everett Collection/Rex Features; **p28** © Bettmann/CORBIS; **p29** © Motoring Picture Library/Alamy; **p32** © Daily Mail/Rex Features; **p33** © Getty Images; **p34-35** © PA Photos; **p34 (tl)** © PAUL MCERLANE/epa/CORBIS; **p36** © Getty Images; **p37** © Condé Nast Archive/CORBIS; **p38-39** © Homer Sykes Archive/Alamy; **p38 (bl)** © Mirrorpix; **p41 (t)** © Homer Sykes Archive/Alamy; **p41 (br)** With thanks to Anne Brocklehurst and Liz Brook; **p42-43** © Getty Images; **p42 (tl)** © Bettmann/CORBIS; **p43 (tr)** © The Sun/ NI Syndication; **p44 (tl)** Lewis Whyld/PA Archive/Press Association Images/Spitting Image Workshop, with thanks to Roger Law; **p45** Neil Munns/PA Archive/Press Association Images; **p46** © PA Photos; **p47** © Redferns; **p48-49** © Rex Features; **p48 (tl)** © M&N/Alamy © Peter Blake. All rights reserved, DACS 2009; **p50-51** © David Hoffman Photo Library/Alamy; **p52-53** © Sipa Press/Rex Features; **p54** © UPP/Topfoto; **p55** © PA Photos; **p56** © Trinity Mirror/Mirrorpix/Alamy; **p57** © Damien Hirst. All rights reserved, DACS 2009; **p58-59** Antony Gormley, *Angel of the North* © the artist/Photo Courtesy Gateshead Metropolitan Borough Council, Photographer Colin Cuthbert; **p60-61** © Touhig Sion/ Corbis Sygma

Additional designs by Stephen Moncrieff
Digital design by John Russell
Picture research by Ruth King